History's Mysteries

GHOST SHIPS,
ARE SHIPS REALLY HAUNTED?

MEGAN COOLEY PETERSON

BLACK RABBIT BOOKS

Bolt is published by Black Rabbit Books
P.O. Box 227, Mankato, Minnesota, 56002.
www.blackrabbitbooks.com

Jen Besel, editor; Grant Gould, designer;
Omay Ayres, photo researcher

Cataloging-in-Publication Data can be found at the Library of Congress.
ISBN 978-1-68072-410-3 (library binding)
ISBN 978-1-64466-257-1 (paperback)
ISBN 978-1-68072-526-1 (ebook)

Image Credits

Alamy: Maciej Bledowski, 20; North Wind Picture Archives, 10; Tithi Luadthong, 8–9; YAY Media AS, 26; digitalcommonwealth.org: A. Ernest Mills, 22 (t), 23 (b); Dreamstime: Padonr, 6; Philcold, Cover (ship); Psychoshadowmaker, 4–5; tuilinntan, 15; iStock: fotokostic, 17; Shutterstock: Anna Om, 25 (moon); Baimieng, 1; Digital Storm, 3; Dmitrydesign, 12–13 (skulls); fixer00, 31; iprachenko, 22–23 (m); Jamilia Marini, 21; Joe Prachatree, 16 (b); makar, 29 (ship); Maria Isaeva, Cover, 29 (magnifying glass); MoreVector, 14–15 (skull); Nerthuz, 25 (ship); Oleg Golovnev, 29 (paper); Rolau Elena, 21; Top Photo Corporation, 16 (t); Triff, 19 (water); tsuneomp, 32; Vecster, 29 (skull); welburnstuart, 19 (ship); villreal.com: Unknown, 12–13 (ship)
Every effort has been made to contact copyright holders for material reproduced in this book. Any omissions will be rectified in subsequent printings if notice is given to the publisher.

CONTENTS

CHAPTER 1

A Ghostly SIGHTING

In 1878, the HMS *Eurydice* was sailing home to England. A blizzard struck. The ship didn't reach **port**. The ship sank, but it didn't disappear. People have claimed to see the ship ever since.

Spotted by a Prince

In 1998, Prince Edward said he saw the *Eurydice*. He was filming a TV show. Suddenly, he spotted a ship on the water. Then, just as suddenly, it vanished. Had the *Eurydice* returned?

Only two crew members survived the *Eurydice* sinking.

CHAPTER 2

STORIES of Ghost Ships

Ghost ships have fascinated people for hundreds of years. These ships are said to sink and return as ghosts. The *Flying Dutchman* is a famous ghost ship. According to **legend**, it sank in the 1600s.

The *Flying Dutchman* was featured in the Pirates of the Caribbean movies.

A Cursed Crew

Stories say the *Dutchman* was **cursed**. Its crew is doomed to sail the seas forever. Many sailors have claimed to see the **phantom** ship. Sighting the *Dutchman* is said to bring bad luck.

A TIMELINE OF SOME *FLYING DUTCHMAN* SIGHTINGS

1600s
***Flying Dutchman* sinks.**

1881
Prince George of Wales spots the ship near Australia.

1939
Swimmers see the ship near South Africa.

1942
Crew members on a ship see the *Dutchman* near South Africa.

2012
A man posts a YouTube video possibly of the *Dutchman* near Wales.

South American Ghost Ship

Off the coast of Chile sails the *Caleuche.* People say this ghost ship carries the spirits of dead people. Witnesses claim to hear music on the ship.

Descriptions of the Fire Ship

burning hull

black shadows on deck

huge ship with gray sails

Phantom Fire Ship

A ghost ship also sails in Chaleur Bay, Canada. This ship is covered in flames. One woman said a ghost from the ship approached her. The ghost was burned and had no legs.

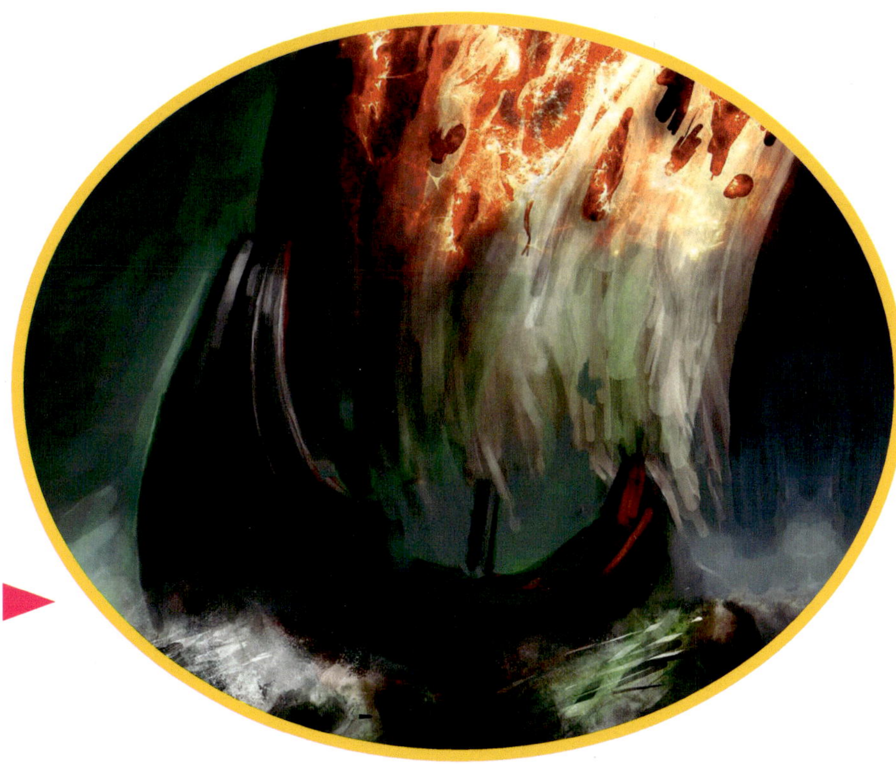

CHAPTER 3

INVESTIGATING Ghost Ships

Are ghost ships real? Or do people only imagine them? Some historians argue the *Flying Dutchman* was probably not even a real ship.

Skeptics say fog or mist could be mistaken for a ghost ship.

Carried by Currents

Other people think science explains ghost ships. Damaged ships don't always sink. In fact, many **abandoned** ships float in the ocean. Ocean **currents** carry these ships around the world.

BECOMING A GHOST SHIP

The *A. Ernest Mills* carried salt. Here's how it became a "ghost ship."

Step 1

The ship crashed into a military destroyer and sank.

Step 2

Salt carried in the ship dissolved in the water.

Step 3

Without the salt's weight, the ship floated back to the surface.

Glowing Gases

Scientists argue Chaleur Bay's fire ship doesn't exist. They say the flames are glowing gases. An **electric charge** makes gases in the air glow. It is visible only in the dark. This could explain why most fire ship sightings happen at night.

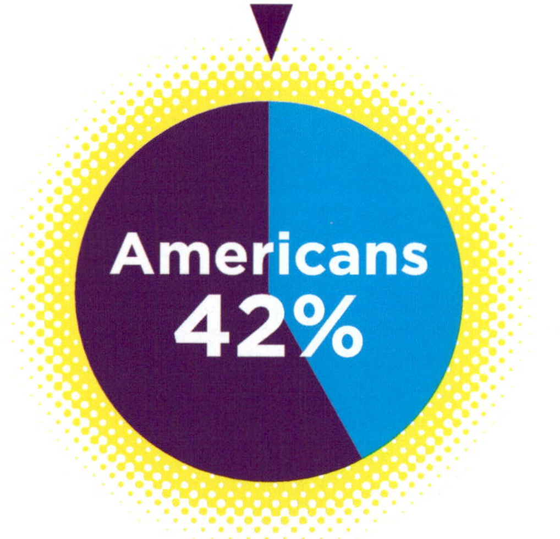

How many believe in ghosts?

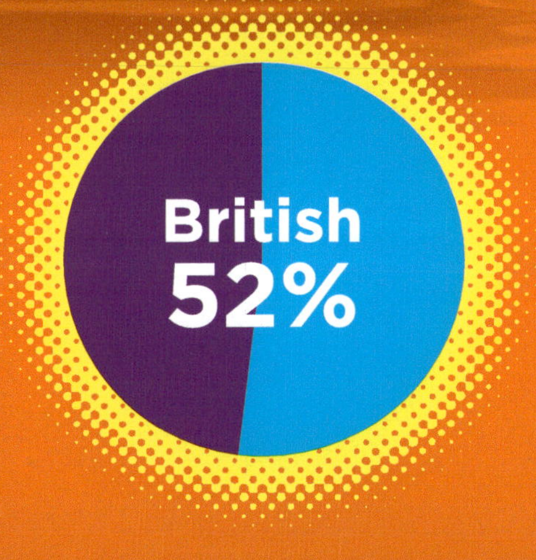

Polls taken in 2013 showed how many people believe in ghosts.

CHAPTER 4

You DECIDE

Sunken ships. Cursed sailors. Many people say ghost ships are real. But others aren't so sure. The mystery may never be solved. But guessing what happened can be spooky fun.

Asking Questions to Solve the Mystery

Researchers ask questions to solve history's mysteries. You can too!

WHO? Who has reported sightings?

WHAT? What research has been done?

WHEN? When did sightings happen?

WHERE? Where do sightings take place?

WHY?

Why are people interested in ghost ships?

HOW?

How could the same boat be seen in several places?

What other questions do you have?

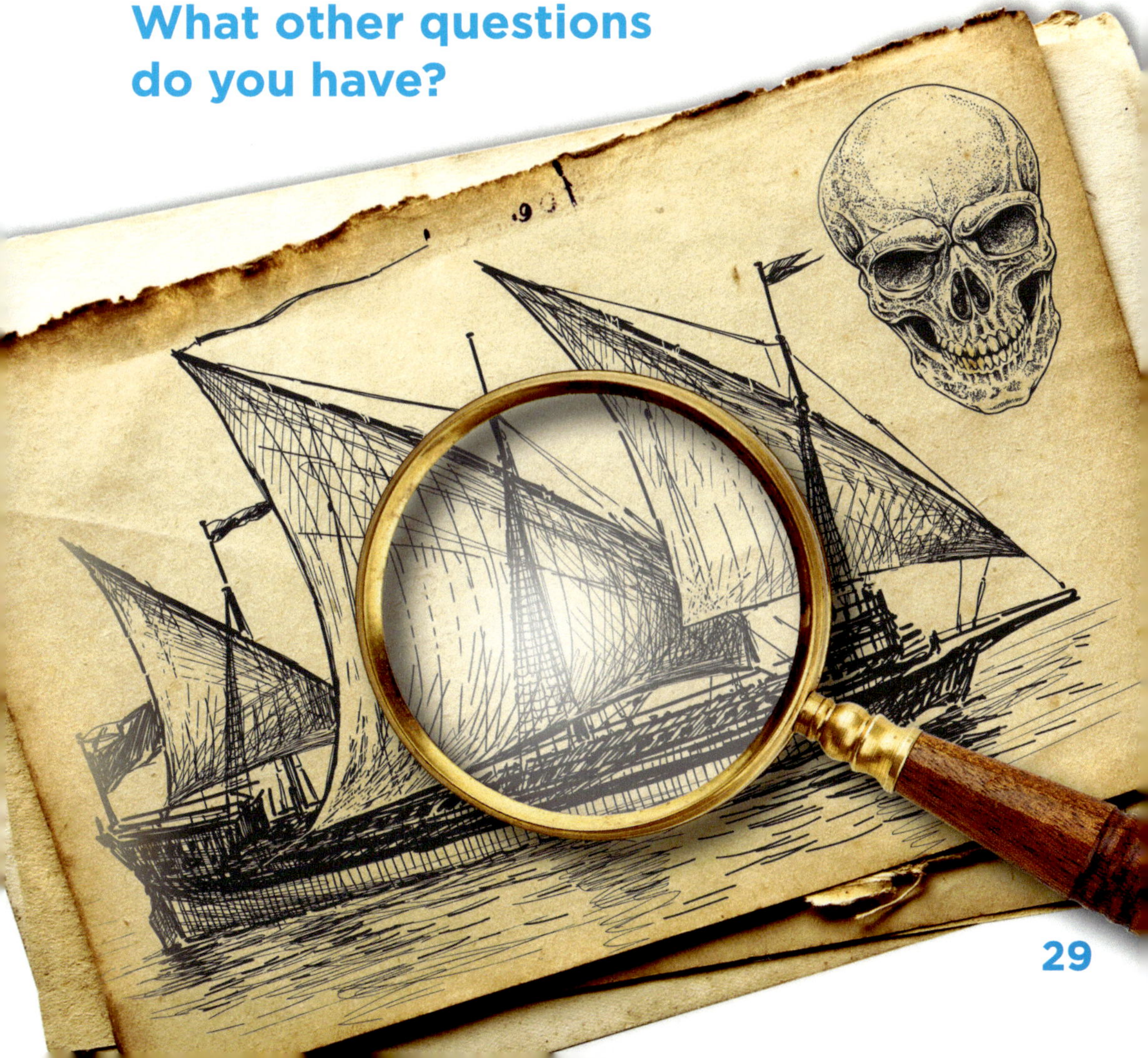

abandon (uh-BAN-duhn)—to leave something and never return to it

current (KUR-uhnt)—the part of a fluid body, such as air or water, moving continuously in a certain direction

cursed (KURST)—to be under an evil spell meant to cause harm

electric charge (e-LEK-trik CHARJ)—the quantity of electricity that is related to the balance of electrons and protons in an object

hull (HUHL)—the main part of a ship or boat, including the deck, sides, and bottom

legend (LEJ-uhnd)—a story from the past that cannot be proven true

phantom (FAN-tuhm)—something that appears to be real but has no physical existence

port (PORT)—a harbor town or city where ships take on or deliver cargo

skeptic (SKEP-tik)—a person who questions everything

BOOKS

Owen, Ruth. *Ghost Ship: The Pharaoh's Buried Vessel.* Egypt's Ancient Secrets. New York: Bearport Publishing, 2017.

Owings, Lisa. *Ghosts at Sea.* Ghost Stories. Minneapolis: Bellwether Media Inc., 2017.

Roland, James. *Frightful Ghost Ships.* Fear Fest. Minneapolis: Lerner Publications, 2017.

WEBSITES

Are Ghost Ships Real?
ed.ted.com/lessons/are-ghost-ships-real-peter-b-campbell

Eerie! 6 Haunting Tales of Ghost Ships
www.livescience.com/48489-tales-of-ghost-ships.html

Stories of the Real Ghost Ships Yet to be Explained
www.hauntedrooms.co.uk/stories-real-ghost-ships-famous-found

INDEX